Sea Secrets

TINY CLUES TO A BIG MYSTERY

Written by Mary M. Cerullo & Beth E. Simmons
Illustrated by Kirsten Carlson

TAYLOR TRADE PUBLISHING
Lanham • Boulder • New York • London

Published by Taylor Trade Publishing
An imprint of The Rowman & Littlefield Publishing Group, Inc.
4501 Forbes Boulevard, Suite 200, Lanham, Maryland 20706
www.rowman.com

Unit A, Whitacre Mews, 26–34 Stannary Street, London SE11 4AB

Distributed by NATIONAL BOOK NETWORK

Text and Illustrations Copyright © 2008, 2015 by
The Regents of the University of California
First Taylor Trade Publishing edition published in 2015
Originally published in 2008 by Moonlight Publishing, Inc. Reprinted by permission.

Book Design by Kirsten Carlson

Library of Congress Control Number: 2014958237

ISBN: 978-0-9779603-9-2 (cloth : alk. paper)
ISBN: 978-1-63076-075-5 (pbk. : alk. paper)
ISBN: 978-1-63076-076-2 (electronic)

About the Long Term Ecological Research (LTER) Network (lternet.edu)

The LTER network is a large-scale program supported by the National Science Foundation.
It consists of 25 ecological research projects, each of which is focused on a different
ecosystem. The goals of the LTER network are:

Understanding: To understand a diverse array of ecosystems at multiple spatial and
temporal scales.

Synthesis: To create general knowledge through long-term, interdisciplinary research,
synthesis of information, and development of theory.

Information: To inform the LTER and broader scientific community by creating well designed
and well documented databases.

Legacies: To create a legacy of well designed and documented long-term observations,
experiments, and archives of samples and specimens for future generations.

Education: To promote training, teaching, and learning about long-term ecological research and
the Earth's ecosystems, and to educate a new generation of scientists.

Outreach: To reach out to the broader scientific community, natural resource managers,
policymakers, and the general public by providing decision support, information, recommendations,
and the knowledge and capability to address complex environmental challenges.

∞™ The paper used in this publication meets the minimum requirements of American National Standard
for Information Sciences—Permanence of Paper for Printed Library Materials, ANSI/NISO Z39.48-1992.

Printed in Yuanzhou, China January 2015

Published in cooperation with the
Long Term Ecological Research Network,
which is funded by the National Science Foundation.

*To the Waterkeepers, who fight to keep
rivers, lakes, and oceans clean. M.C.*

To my beautiful girls Morgan and Kiera. B.S.

*To the plankton—
they are small, amazing,
and extremely significant. K.C.*

Mysterious changes are happening in the world's oceans. Scientists are looking for clues to unravel these mysteries. Sometimes it's the smallest things that turn out to be the most important…

Where are the seabirds?

Off the California coast, the rocky Farallon Islands rise above the surface of the Pacific Ocean. The islands are sometimes quiet. But for a short time each spring and summer, they become an area for hundreds of thousands of Cassin's auklets to raise their families. Among the seabirds that visit the island, the chubby Cassin's auklets return to the same mate and the same nest on the island year after year to lay their eggs.

Once the eggs hatch, the parents take turns flying out to the open ocean, where they may dive 100 feet (30 m) into the water to find food for their chicks.

In May and June, there are often hundreds of hungry chicks squawking loudly for their parents. Today it is strangely quiet.

There is only one nest with a chick among 400 empty nests. It appears the birds abandoned their nests this year.

The waters surrounding these islands are famous as the hunting grounds of the great white shark. Surfers in nearby San Francisco keep alert for a tall fin slicing through the water. But the scientists who study the auklets know that the giant sharks didn't drive the birds from their nests. What did?

Cassin's Auklet *Ptychoramphus aleuticus*
Habitat Range: Eastern Pacific Ocean

Thirty years ago, scientists counted 105,000 Cassin's auklets on the Farallon Islands. Now there are 25,000.

Where are the whales?

The deep, loud song of a blue whale echoes through the water just off the California coast. He is calling to a female, who may be more than a hundred miles away.

Scientists studying blue whales around the world have found they sing different types of songs, depending on where they live. Nine different groups of blue whales have been identified, each with its own unique song.

Blue whales feed in cold waters, like those along the coast of California and the Southern Ocean that surrounds Antarctica. There, both male and female blue whales make moaning sounds similar to those an elephant makes. Perhaps they are calling the other whales to tell them where the food is.

Once, 250,000 blue whales roamed the oceans. Today there are fewer than 5,000.

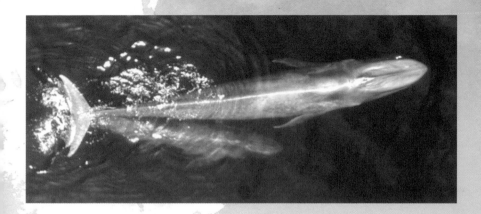

Blue Whale *Balaenoptera musculus*
Habitat Range: Oceans worldwide

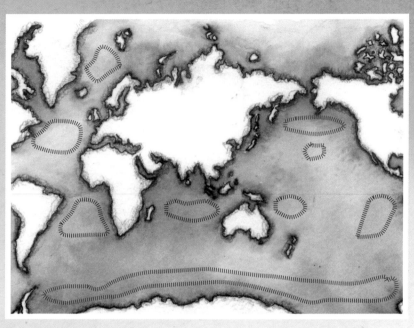

|||||||||| winter breeding range
|||||||||| summer feeding range

Blue whales, the largest animals that have ever lived on earth, eat tons of food each day.

You would think the giant blue whales would be king of the seas. But scientists have found that the groups of whales are smaller. What's happening to them?

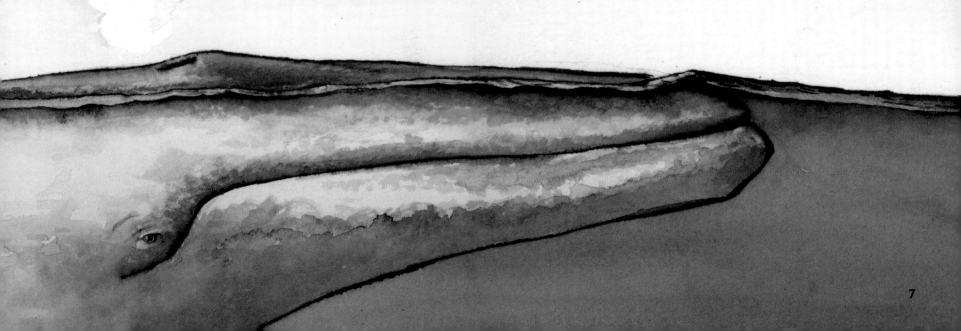

Where are the penguins?

At the northern edge of the Antarctic continent is the western Antarctic Peninsula. It is surrounded by ice for much of the year. Flightless black and white Adélie penguins spend their winters here on sea ice. These large blocks of moving ice allow the birds to find their food and fatten up for the nesting season to come.

Adélie parents build pebble nests for their young in October, the start of spring on the Antarctic Peninsula. Once the two or three eggs hatch, mothers and fathers take turns getting food for their chicks. A group of parents marches across the ice, usually in a single file, to the open water. At the ice edge they wait for the others to catch up, then they leap as a group into the frigid ocean. This makes it harder for leopard seals and killer whales waiting just offshore to gobble them up.

The penguins' troubles aren't over once they've escaped their predators. A change is making many Adélie penguins leave this nesting ground. Many of them are building new nests farther south, where it is colder. Scientists want to know why.

Adélie Penguin *Pygoscelis adeliae*
Habitat Range: Antarctic Ocean

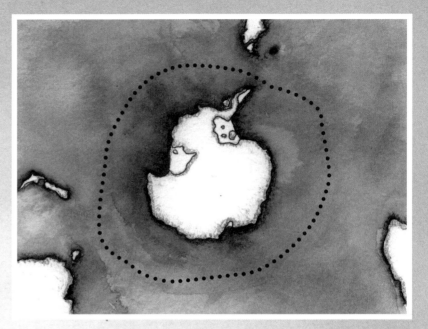

Only a quarter as many Adélie penguins live on the western Antarctic Peninsula as there were 40 years ago.

A Scientific Detective Story

Why are these animals changing their habits?
Can you find a connection among all three animals?

Scientists are collecting clues to try to find the answers. You and the scientists must gather evidence like any good detective.

Finding answers in the ocean can be challenging because it's such a large body of salt water. The Pacific, for example, is the largest of the world's five oceans, covering over 60 million square miles (15.5 trillion sq km). (That's 15 times the size of the United States!) Ocean animals like the seabirds in the California Current, the penguins in the Antarctic Peninsula waters, and the blue whales that swim in both areas, live far apart. Studying animals that live far from each other tells scientists a lot about the health of such a large ecosystem.

Many scientists are doing *Long-Term Ecological Research* to find out more about ocean ecosystems. The work, or research, these scientists do is called "long term" because it often takes longer than weeks or months. Sometimes it takes years and years to find the answers they are looking for.

Let's begin along the California coast.

Do you have what it takes to be a scientific detective?

Identifying great mysteries in the natural world and having a sense of wonder are part of science. Ask questions, observe, and experiment with the world around you!

Cassin's Auklet Research ●

Blue Whale Research ●

PACIFIC OCEAN

Adélie Penguin Research ●
Blue Whale Research ●

Explore and Collect the Clues

Cassin's Auklet

It's a bright, sunny day off the coast of San Francisco and scientists have landed on a small island to study Cassin's auklets. Sarah's dad is one of the scientists, and today Sarah is helping. It's the spring nesting season, and Sarah's task is to count auklet parents, eggs, and chicks.

She slowly makes her way along the rocky shore, looking inside hidden spots where the auklets like to nest. But she isn't finding many birds.

Her dad is helping to capture and band the few birds they have found on the island today. They place a band with a code number around each bird's leg. Then, when the researchers come back next spring, they will check the bands of birds they capture to find out if the same auklets are returning to the island.

For 35 years, scientists have been doing "bird counts" to tell them how the population of Cassin's auklets changes from year to year. Some years, they counted thousands of chicks. In some recent years, there were none. Sarah is hoping her dad and the other researchers can find out why few chicks are here this year.

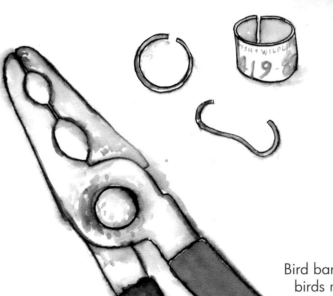

Bird banding helps scientists learn where birds migrate, as well as how they continue to live in the wild.

SAN FRANCISCO

LOS ANGELES

SAN DIEGO

200 MILES

322 KM

Blue Whale

Out in the ocean, another team of researchers is tracking a blue whale. It isn't easy, because whales spend most of their time underwater. But with patience, there is a way. Whales need air, so they have to come to the surface to breathe. That is the scientists' best chance of getting information about these massive animals.

Erin is studying to become an oceanographer, and this is only her second whale tracking expedition. But today Erin has the most important job of the entire team.

The boat trolls along near a blue whale just under the water's surface. Suddenly, the whale comes up for air. Erin is ready. She attaches a bioacoustic probe — a suction cup device that records water temperature, how deep the whale dives, and how far it travels. That way, the team can record the sights and sounds of the whale's journey.

Erin attaches the equipment just as the giant whale slips back underwater. Her crewmates give her high fives. She hopes that what they learn from this whale will help them understand how the blue whales live and how they might adapt to changes in the ocean.

The song of the coastal blue whales near the California Current is more complex than the song of their blue whale cousins living south of the equator around the Antarctic Peninsula. Whales that swim in the southern hemisphere feed on plankton near sea·ice. Even when northern and southern whales migrate for breeding and feeding, they don't cross the equator.

Adélie Penguin

A third group of scientific detectives braves the weather in Antarctica. Joe and Maria are using gray duct tape to attach tiny backpacks to Adélie penguins. The birds struggle and try to nip the researchers, but once the backpacks are in place, the penguins don't even seem to notice them.

Inside the backpacks are transmitters called Platform Terminal Transmitters (PTTs) that allow the scientists to follow the birds' journey offshore. The radio signals sent back

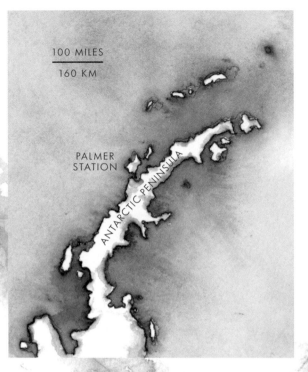

to Joe and Maria tell them that the Adélie penguins swim 10 miles (16 km) or more to reach deep underwater canyons. When the penguins return, Joe and Maria pump water into their stomachs. This makes the penguins throw up, so the researchers can see what the birds ate when they were in the canyons.

Joe and Maria collect the goopy pink and gray mess in plastic bags and put the bags in a freezer. They will take them back to the lab to study. They're hoping what they learn will give them some clues about why the Adélies are moving farther south.

The information from these backpacks on penguins gets sent to a satellite and then delivered to scientists almost instantly.

ZipNGO® BRAND BAGS

#3

Carlson
A PENGVN CO
UNE PENGU NO EN

Discovery

Have you ever heard the saying "It's in the details?"
For scientists, that's definitely true. It means that you have
to consider everything — even small things that might not
seem very important.

If you look at who eats what in an ocean food web, you
might be surprised to find that even the tiniest speck of life
has a huge impact on everything else. For instance, the blue
whale — the "granddaddy" of them all — feeds on some of
the littlest creatures in the ocean.

"Look at the big picture" is another saying. If you study
penguins, you should also know a lot about Antarctica, the
climate, the oceans, and other animals there. Together, all
this information helps you see how everything is connected.
So if you discover a new fact about the Adélie penguin,
other scientists may ask themselves, "What does this mean
for other ocean animals?"

The researchers of Cassin's auklets, blue whales, and Adélie penguins compared notes and made a surprising discovery. From off the California coast to Antarctica, through the Northern and Southern Pacific Ocean, these animals living so far apart have one thing that links them together. They all eat the same food: krill.

Blue whales can survive on a steady diet of these tiny creatures. One scientist estimated that a blue whale eats about 6,000 pounds (2,700 kg) of krill each day.

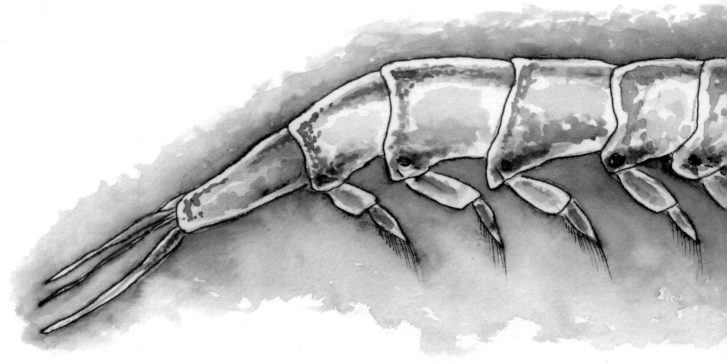

What Are Krill?

If you've never heard of krill, you're not the only one. What are they? Where are they? How many are there? If three groups of animals that eat krill are changing, it's likely that something is going on with krill. Now it's your turn to do the research. Your mission is to find out what it is.

But first, you'll need to know what you're looking for. Krill are shrimp-like creatures, both in size and looks. Krill have hard shells, like their other

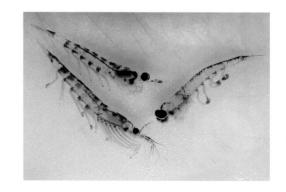

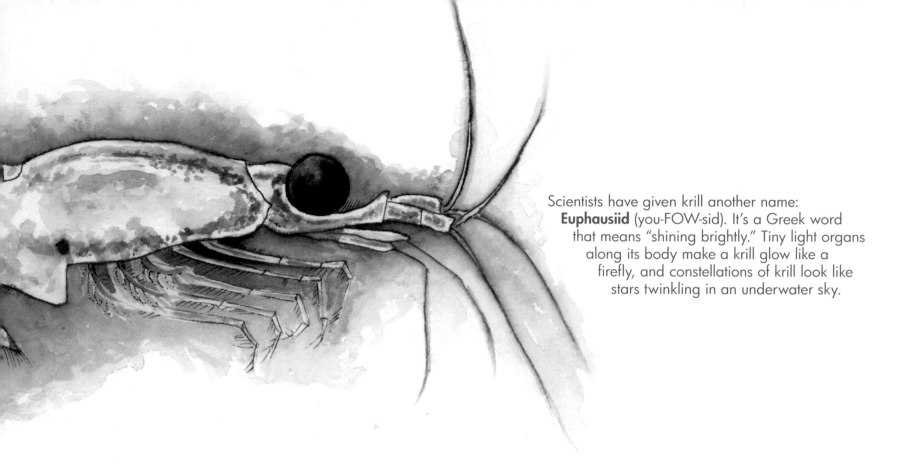

Scientists have given krill another name: **Euphausiid** (you-FOW-sid). It's a Greek word that means "shining brightly." Tiny light organs along its body make a krill glow like a firefly, and constellations of krill look like stars twinkling in an underwater sky.

crustacean relatives: crabs, lobsters, crayfish, and shrimp. Krill's shells are mostly clear, with small spots of red. How big is a krill compared to you? The largest one, which lives in Antarctica, is about the size of your thumb.

So where do you go to find krill? They are found in every ocean, but let's investigate the krill in the California Current ecosystem, and the krill that live along the western Antarctic Peninsula. If we can find out what is happening with these krill, we might find the answers to our mystery.

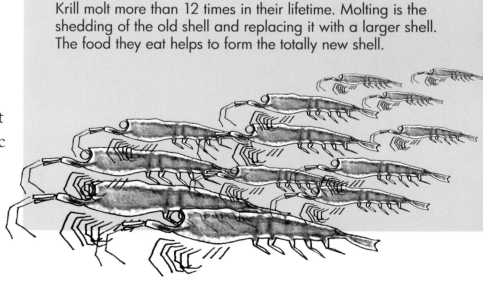

Krill molt more than 12 times in their lifetime. Molting is the shedding of the old shell and replacing it with a larger shell. The food they eat helps to form the totally new shell.

Common name:
Pacific krill

Scientific name:
Euphausia pacifica

Adult length:
0.5–1 inch (11—25 mm)

Maximum age:
2 years

Diet:
phytoplankton & microzooplankton

Habitat range:
Pacific Ocean from California to Japan

To escape danger, krill flick their tails to zip backwards through the water, traveling as fast as three feet a second (0.8m/s).

First stop, the California Current.

You'll need a submarine to track krill here because they hang out 650 to 1,300 feet (200–400 m) down. Or, like the scientists do, you can lower a special piece of equipment called a bongo net to catch krill at different depths in the ocean. Krill travel up and down in the cold water between day and night to find food and to avoid predators. Scientists discovered they do this every day, swimming up to a half mile!

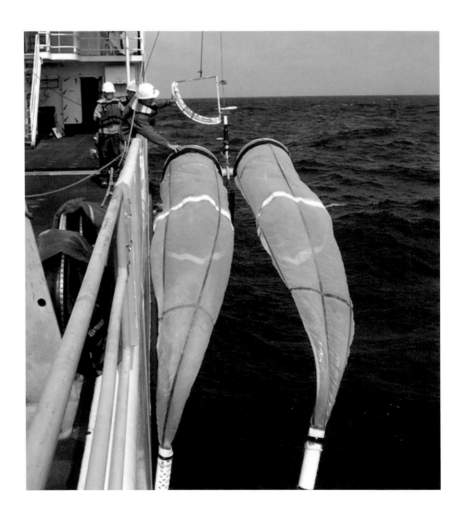

Next stop, the Antarctic Peninsula.

Hop a plane heading south and we'll check out the Antarctic krill next. Before you dive into the icy water to see these krill in action, you'll need a diving suit, a mask, a scuba tank, and some courage.

Here krill gather close to the ocean's surface in such huge groups that their shells sometimes turn the water pink. You will be surrounded by unimaginably large numbers of krill, called *swarms*. There have been sightings of krill swarms more than 7 miles (11.6 km) across. That's estimated at 2.5 *trillion* krill. Scientists discuss many possible reasons krill form large swarms. For example, Antarctic krill may group together to protect themselves from predators.

Common name:

Antarctic krill

Scientific name:
Euphausia superba

Adult length:
1.3–2.5 inches (33–65 mm)

Maximum age:
5–7 years

Diet:
phytoplankton & microzooplankton

Habitat range:
Waters surrounding Antarctica

There are eighty-six different kinds of krill that live from warm, tropical seas to the polar oceans.

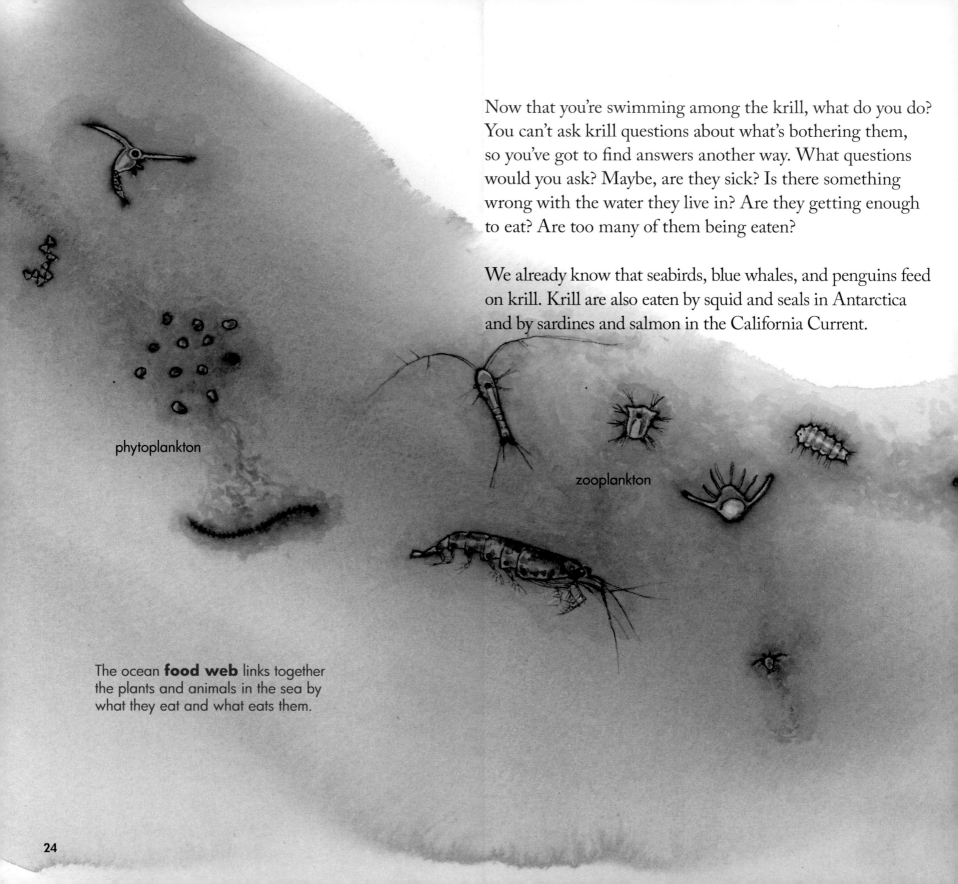

Now that you're swimming among the krill, what do you do? You can't ask krill questions about what's bothering them, so you've got to find answers another way. What questions would you ask? Maybe, are they sick? Is there something wrong with the water they live in? Are they getting enough to eat? Are too many of them being eaten?

We already know that seabirds, blue whales, and penguins feed on krill. Krill are also eaten by squid and seals in Antarctica and by sardines and salmon in the California Current.

phytoplankton

zooplankton

The ocean **food web** links together the plants and animals in the sea by what they eat and what eats them.

Krill are probably the target of many sea creatures because they're nutritious and plentiful — an easy meal!

So what do krill eat? It's hard to see what krill are eating because they feed on tiny green plants called *phytoplankton* (FIE-toe-plank-ton). The plants float near the surface to get the sunlight they need to grow. Krill also feed on very small animals called *zooplankton* (ZOE-plank-ton) that you need a microscope to see. The front legs of krill form a food basket which collects microscopic plankton from the ocean water.

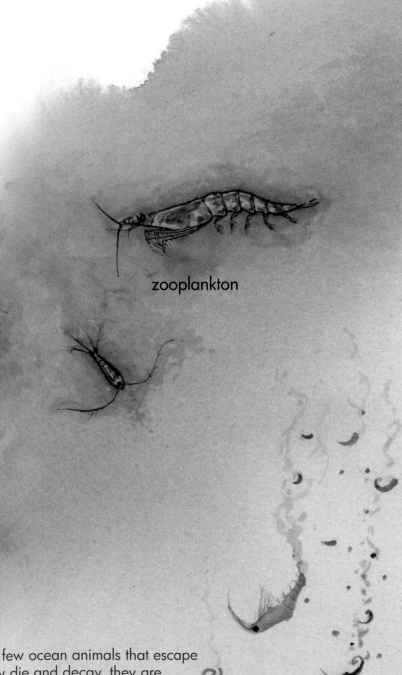

zooplankton

phytoplankton

Detritus

What happens to those few ocean animals that escape being eaten? When they die and decay, they are recycled into ingredients that nourish phytoplankton, much like fertilizers help flowers bloom on land.

Be an Oceanographer

Sample the ocean water and take a closer look:

Water temperature?
Slightly warmer than previous records.

Water clarity? Not too bad.

Krill's food supply? Running low!

And why is that?
Hmmm…
let's take another look at your notes,
starting with water temperature.

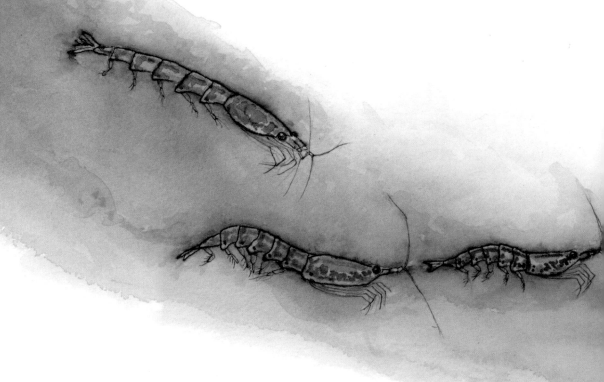

Scientists know that the oceans have been getting warmer. In the past 50 years, winter air temperatures on the Antarctic peninsula have risen more than 10 °F (6 °C). That causes ice to melt, and the phytoplankton living under the ice are losing their home. Fewer phytoplankton means less food for krill.

In the last 50 years, the California Current water temperature has warmed 2 to 5 °F (about 1–3 °C). In order to grow well in the Pacific, phytoplankton need cool, nutrient-rich water to come up from the ocean depths. This is called upwelling. But upwelling doesn't happen as much when the surface water warms up. So the krill's food supply is changing here, too.

What's the big deal? After all, a temperature change of a few degrees doesn't bother us. But for some animals, a small change in temperature will require a large change in how or where the animals live. This is called an adaptation. Sometimes animals must make a change in order to survive. That's why some animals are starting to look in other places for food.

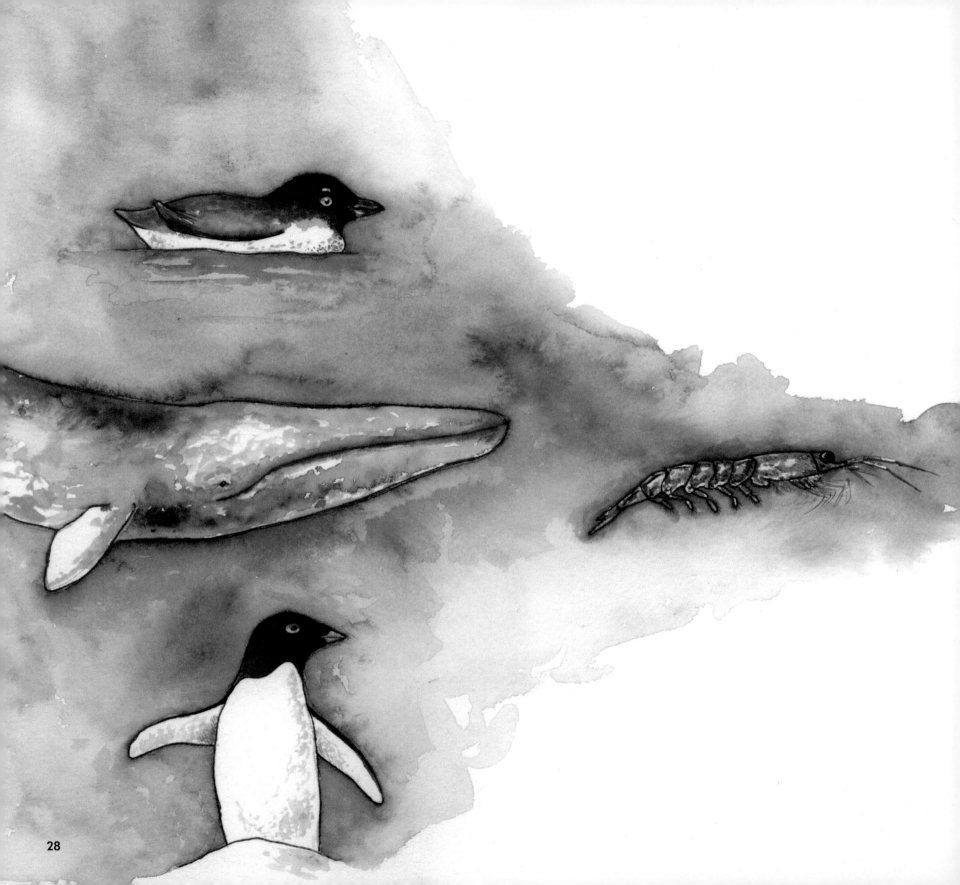

Small Creatures with a Big Message

In what may seem like a tiny detail — a change of a few degrees — we see how the entire ocean food web is affected. Cassin's auklets are unable to return to their old nests to have their chicks when their prey has moved too far out to sea. Fewer Adélies are returning to the Antarctic Peninsula to build their nests and raise their chicks because ice is melting and food is harder to find. Blue whale groups are getting smaller as some whales are swimming farther in search of a meal.

What are krill telling us?

Krill can't talk but what they are telling us speaks volumes about how life across thousands of miles in the sea is connected. Theirs is a story of how one species can impact communities of animals across an entire ecosystem. Directly and indirectly, krill are a visible link among phytoplankton and whales, birds and their babies, and penguins on the peninsula. If climate warming is impacting phytoplankton production in the ocean's food web, then krill's food supply is changing too. In some places krill are disappearing. In others, they are showing up at different times of the year. Many krill are doing just fine.

In a voice as big as the ocean, krill are reminding us to change our habits, as our lives are linked to the ocean. Let us continue to investigate ocean mysteries and develop a better consciousness of our individual practices, preserving the planet for everyone.

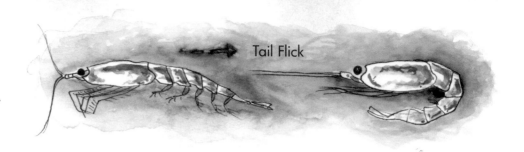
Tail Flick

CONNECT THE CLUES

Match the terms and illustrations to krill characteristics.

Krill Eye

Bongo Net

Krill Swarm

1. Krill may group together to stay safe. You might find as many as 100,000 per cubic meter of ocean water, sometimes turning the water pink. This safety-in-numbers strategy protects krill.

2. Young krill escape with high-speed swimming and acrobatic maneuvers to escape becoming food for larger animals.

3. This instrument is used by scientists to observe small krill. Some of their tiny features cannot be seen with the naked eye.

4. Krill are named for a Greek word that means "shining brightly." This adaptation allows them to attract a mate, interact with other krill, or hide the shape of their body in open water.

5. This large collecting tool is used by scientists to gather zooplankton samples throughout the ocean from deep water all the way up to the surface.

6. A strategy used by many crustaceans, including krill, is to shrink in size as a way to use less body energy.

7. The two of these on krill are sensitive to light and help them get around in dark waters of the ocean.

8. Krill have developed front legs that together form a bucket that helps them collect microscopic plankton in the ocean water.

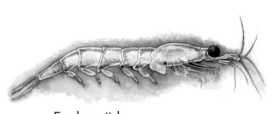
Euphausiid

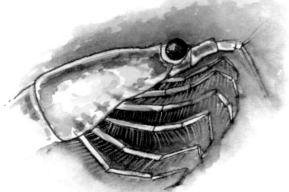
Krill Food Basket

Krill Molting

Microscope

GLOSSARY

adapt   to change

banding   a method of identifying animals so they can be found later

bongo net   a piece of equipment that helps scientists catch plankton at different depths

California Current   a southward-moving ocean current that runs along the coast of California

crustaceans   a group of ocean animals having a hard shell, such as lobsters, crayfish, and shrimp

detritus   dead plants and animals that are recycled into food for other animals

ecosystem   a community of plants, animals, and their surroundings

food web   links together the plants and animals under the sea by what they eat and what eats them

krill   shrimp-like creatures

microscope   a tool that helps view objects that are too small to be seen with your eye

molting   the shedding of an old shell by the replacement of a larger shell

nutrient   a nourishing substance

oceanographer   a person who studies the ocean

peninsula   land surrounded by water on three sides

phytoplankton   microscopic plants that drift with the currents

population   the number of a particular kind of living thing

predators   animals that feed on other animals

prey   animals hunted or caught for food

radio transmitter   an electric device that sends information to a recordiing device located far away

sea ice   frozen ocean water

species   a specific kind of living thing

swarm   very large number of similar animals

trillion   one million million; 1,000,000,000,000,000,000,000,000

upwelling   cold, deep water rich in nutrients that comes up to the ocean's surface

zooplankton   small, drifting animals that feed on phytoplankton or other zooplankton

Acknowledgements

A book like this does not get written without leaving debt to others that must be recognized. Lead scientists Mark Ohman whose patience and vast knowledge of the subject helped to inspire the story. Hugh Ducklow, Langdon Quetin, Robin Ross and Bill Fraser who offered their invaluable insight, and expertise about Antarctica and its science. Kristen McCurry whose editorial input helped us not only meet our deadline but also shape up our story.

A number of our colleagues were willing to contribute to the project through interviews. They not only reviewed the manuscript and provided feedback, but also gave support, guidance and photographs. Bill Sydeman, Ph.D., Director of the Farallon Institute, Melissa Pitkin, Education and Outreach Director from Point Reyes Bird Observatory, www.prbo.org, and the Farallon National Wildlife Refuge, Erin Oleson of Scripps Institution of Oceanography, Donna Fraser of Polar Ocean Research Group, Moira Decima of Scripps Institution of Oceanography, William Burgess Ph.D., Senior Research Engineer at Greeneridge Sciences, Inc. for the whale tagging photograph, NOAA National Marine Fisheries Southwest Fisheries Science Center for the use of the blue whale mother and her calf photograph. To both LTER sites the California Current Ecosystem (CCE) and Palmer Station (PAL) for their resources and support. Thank you to DES for his encouragement and tolerance during this project and all its demands. To Mary and Kirsten for their experience, patience and friendship.

Support for this book was provided by the Schoolyard Program of the Long-Term Ecological Research (SLTER) program. The SLTER is funded by the National Science Foundation (award numbers 0217282 and OCE 0417616). Additional funding awarded through the LTER Children's Book Series Fund.

LONG TERM ECOLOGICAL RESEARCH NETWORK

The National Science Foundation's LTER network began in 1980 and includes 26 field sites across a wide range of the North American continent, including the Caribbean islands, the Pacific, and even Antarctica. Research covers a diverse array of the Earth's ecosystems from deserts and estuaries, lakes, oceans, and coral reefs to prairies, forests, the alpine, and the Arctic tundra: www.lternet.edu.

The LTER network goals focus:

- To **understand** a diverse array of ecosystems at multiple spatial and temporal scales.

- To create general knowledge through long-term, interdisciplinary research, **synthesis** of information, and the development of theory.

- To **inform** the LTER and broader scientific community through the creation of effectively documented databases.

- To create a **legacy** of well-designed and documented long-term observations, experiments, and archives of samples and specimens for future generations.

- To promote the training, teaching, and learning about long-term ecological research and the earth's ecosystems, and to **educate** a new generation of scientists.

- To **reach out** to the broader scientific community, natural resource managers, policy makers, and the general public by providing decision support, information, recommendations, and the knowledge and capability to address complex environmental challenges.

In 1993, the LTER network in the United States was joined by at least 30 other countries forming the International Long Term Ecological Research (ILTER) Network: www.ilternet.edu. The goal is to meet the growing need for global communication and collaboration among long-term ecological researchers by assessing and resolving complex environmental issues together.

In 1998, LTER developed an initiative for all 26 sites to embrace a Schoolyard Program to enhance learning for K – 12 students in both formal and informal learning communities. *Sea Secrets*, along with the other children's books in the Schoolyard Book Series, are examples of a broad-scale, long-term effort to combine scientific research and science education: http://schoolyard.lternet.edu.

Sea Secrets: Tiny Clues to a Big Mystery website: http://cce.lternet.edu/outreach/seasecrets/ provides free access to teaching and learning resources. It showcases artwork, educational materials, and additional photography from both LTER sites. It also houses an activity guide that elaborates on many of the complex science topics covered within the book. This guide is a growing collection of activities, experiments, case studies and fact sheets for kids, students, teachers and parents.